RESCUE 911 ™

Humorous Rescues

by R. M. Ferrara

A TRUMPET CLUB ORIGINAL BOOK

The stories in this book are based on actual events as depicted on RESCUE 911®.

If 9-1-1 isn't the emergency number in your area, learn the emergency numbers used where you live, and post them by each phone.

Special Thanks to
Arnold Shapiro Productions

Published by The Trumpet Club, Inc.,
a subsidiary of Bantam Doubleday Dell Publishing Group, Inc.,
1540 Broadway, New York, New York 10036.

© 1995 CBS Inc.
All rights reserved. The Trumpet Club is an authorized user.
All photographs are the property of RESCUE 911®
and/or are used by permission.

ISBN 0-440-83009-5

Printed in the United States of America
September 1995
3 5 7 9 10 8 6 4 2

Contents

*for Stewart and Karen and Jonathan
and David*

Introduction

Humorous rescues? You may wonder what could possibly be funny about a call to 911. After all, calling 911 is what you do when you are in an emergency situation. Let's say you and a friend are playing in your backyard. Your friend is suddenly stung by a bee, falls to the ground, and seems to be unconscious. You need help right away. What should you do? You should quickly dial 911 or your local emergency number which should be posted on your telephone. At the other end of that call are trained professionals, ready to rush an emergency medical team to your house to help your friend—to save his life! There's nothing funny about that, is there?

No, there's nothing humorous about an emergency rescue—until the rescue is complete, everyone involved is safe and happy, and we can look back to see what caused the crisis. Sometimes people act in ways that seem silly to an outsider. Or they get themselves into ridiculous situations, and can't get themselves out again. What they do or say may make perfect sense to them at the time, but to someone else their actions may seem funny. Being a trained emergency medical worker means that you must quickly assess the situation and then take the appropriate action to rescue anyone and everyone in need. There is no time then to see the humor in the often outrageous predicaments that people's actions cause.

But what about the would-be crook who got caught in the chimney of the house he was trying to rob? Or the art students who almost applied a plaster-of-Paris mask *permanently*? We're getting ahead of ourselves here, but you can see that sometimes people do very funny things and, once they have been safely extricated, everyone involved can look back and laugh.

Read on to see the crazy things that rescue workers have witnessed while helping people. But please keep in mind that dialing 911 is a very serious matter. The service is there for emergency help when you need it. If your area doesn't have 911 service, learn the proper emergency numbers to dial and post them by your phone.

Now, let the fun begin!

Santa Claus?

Imagine being awakened in the middle of the night by a loud noise in your living room, only to find a grown man trapped in your chimney! Sounds like the stories about Santa Claus that we all hear when we're growing up, doesn't it? That's exactly what happens in this story.

January 4, 1993, began quietly in Oceanside, California. Tired after all their holiday activities, Margie and Lawrence Beavers were, like their neighbors, sleeping soundly in their beds. Suddenly, at about 2 AM, they were awakened by a loud noise in their house.

Still half asleep, Margie, 56, got out of bed and made her way to the front door, thinking that someone was knocking. On her way through the living room, Margie was startled to

1

find that the noise was coming from their own living-room fireplace. She called Larry, 62, to join her, and they cautiously approached their hearth, only to find a man's soot-covered head and shoulders suspended above the iron grate of the cold chimney hearth. When they asked the man who he was, he angrily replied, "Santa Claus!" Margie then asked him, "Well, if you're Santa Claus, then where are our presents? We know that we've been good!"

Larry and Margie saw that the man could not move—he was stuck fast, hanging upside down, in their fireplace. He seemed to be okay—he was able to talk to them—but he could move neither up nor down. They had no idea who he was or why he was halfway in their living room, but they were frightened and knew that they needed to get him out of the chimney as quickly as possible. They were extremely curious about the man, and how he came to be in their chimney, but they knew their first priority was getting him safely out.

Still wearing her pajamas, and with their Christmas tree lights blinking in the background, Margie called 911 and explained their unusual situation to Laura Harris, the Oceanside Police Department dispatcher. Laura's first reaction was disbelief. She couldn't understand why or how a man could be trapped in the Beavers' chimney. Her duty log for that night lists the call as a burglary, and as "a man stuck in a chimney." She remembers thinking that usually break-in calls require the police to chase a suspect around the neighborhood. In this case, however, the suspect was right there, ripe for the picking!

Following established procedure, she passed the information about the call to Reggie Grisby, the watch commander for the night. Reggie chuckled when he reviewed the case. Reggie had to struggle to remain professional and not to laugh when he put out the call to police cars in the area. Police officer Katherine Held was about a mile away from the Beavers' house when she got the call. She, too, thought the call might be some kind of joke, but immediately rushed to the house.

When she pulled up in front of their home with her lights flashing, Officer Held was met in the front yard by Margie Beavers. Although the call sounded funny to the rescue squad, it was no joke to Margie and Larry Beavers. They'd been abruptly awakened, and their house had been invaded by a strange man. Margie led Officer Held into the living room, where the man continued to talk nonstop under the watchful eye of Larry Beavers. Officer Held's reaction was one of amazement. She remembers thinking that the whole event would have been perfect for an episode of *Candid Camera*. She questioned the man, and was relieved to find that he was unarmed. But, she couldn't get a straight answer out of him as to why he was in that chimney.

Officer Held called for backup, and arranged to have the Oceanside Fire Department called in to help. Police Officer Brad Hunter arrived and could not help laughing. He asked the stuck man what he had planned to do when he got into the house, and the suspect replied that he intended to "steal the piano!" When Fire Captain Jim Myers arrived on the scene, he was dumbfounded by what he saw. He sent his crew to the roof to see if there was any way to pull the man back out of the chimney from the top. When they found that the only way to get him out was through the hearth, they called for a rescue truck. Then, while the stranger talked nonstop, complaining about how long it was taking the rescue crews to help him, they began to chip away at the Beavers' fireplace.

Margie and Larry, meanwhile, were beginning to relax. Although they were upset, the reactions of the rescue team helped them to see the funny aspects of their situation. While rescue workers took apart their hearth, brick by brick, Margie got out her camera and took a few pictures of the stranger hanging upside down in their living room.

When at last the final brick holding him in place had been removed, the man slipped down into the room. Fire Captain Jim Myers compared the scene to the birth of a baby. He thought that this man must be the dumbest criminal ever, for his plan had failed miserably. Not only was he not able to rob the Beavers, but he had ended up suspended upside down in their living room for approximately two hours! Once he was out and on his feet again, he tried to fight the officers and resist arrest, but they were able to quickly subdue him. The police officers led him out of the house and brought him to the station house for booking. The Beavers finally had their house back to themselves!

The suspect claimed that he had jumped down the Beavers' chimney in an effort to hide from a group of people who were chasing him. He was eventually found guilty of burglary.

As for the Beavers, they'll never think about Santa Claus delivering his presents in quite the same way again! They are able to look back at that wild night now and realize how funny the

As firefighters try to help, the criminal hangs upside down in the chimney. His head is just visible inside the fireplace.

whole escapade really was. They are grateful to the Oceanside Police Department and Fire Department for protecting them and, at the same time, rescuing the criminal. The Beavers know that they have a very funny holiday story to tell their children and grandchildren for years to come. They have made Christmas cards with a picture of the would-be thief hanging upside down in their chimney, with the words, "Just drop in any time!"

Fascinating Facts

- A chimney sweep is a worker who cleans the soot out of chimneys.

- Some modern industrial chimneys are more than 300 feet tall!

- Until the 1800s, people pictured Santa Claus as a tall, thin, dignified man. It wasn't until 1809 that the American author Washington Irving described him as fat and jolly.

Saving Face

If you were an artist, what would you be willing to sacrifice for your craft? Two art students in Lincoln, Nebraska, almost had to find out—the hard way!

Eric Lunde and Dan Potter were students at Union College in Lincoln, Nebraska. As a project for an art class they were taking, they wanted to make plaster masks of their faces. They had seen other students make face casts and thought the masks would be fun things to have. They liked the idea of having their faces permanently captured in the stone-like plaster of Paris. They approached their teacher, Professor Jim McClelland, with the idea, and he agreed to help them. He had helped many students before this with the same sort of project, and anticipated no problems with Eric and Dan's request. They agreed that they would meet in the campus art room around 1 PM on April 16, 1992.

When they met, Professor McClelland first showed the two young men how to mix the plaster of Paris, which would then be applied to their faces, one at a time. They all agreed that Eric's face would be the first one "molded," so they prepared him for the procedure. They began by coating his face with petroleum jelly. This is an essential first step, because the petroleum jelly acts as an agent to keep the plaster of Paris from sticking to hair or skin. Once Eric's face was completely covered with the slippery substance, two specially adapted straws were inserted into his nostrils, to give him a clear airway during the procedure. The plaster would need approximately fifteen minutes to set, at which time the mask could be pulled from Eric's face. The resulting image would be a clear likeness of his face, cast in plaster.

With their initial preparations complete, Eric lay down on a worktable and Professor McClelland and Dan placed a special wooden frame around his head. The frame would hold any excess plaster. When he was comfortable, they began to pour wet plaster over his face.

Eric remembers this as being a very strange sensation. He notes that he had a brief moment of panic, but then—realizing that he could breathe easily—he relaxed. When his face was completely covered with plaster, Professor McClelland and Dan sat down to wait the required fifteen minutes to allow the plaster to dry and set completely.

At the end of the allotted time, they tested the plaster mask, felt that it was hard, and had Eric sit up. When they tried to gently pull the mask away from his face, however, they were shocked to hear his cries of discomfort. Evidently the mask wasn't slipping easily; it appeared to be stuck to his face! They continued to tug gently, but Eric's muffled moans stopped them. Eric noted later that it felt as though his "whole scalp was going to be pulled off!"

High school student Kathy Long happened to walk by the art room at this time. Although she was still in high school, Kathy was taking a few courses at the college. She was also training to become an Emergency Medical Technician (an EMT). She remembers thinking about her training, trying to recall if anything she had already learned could be applied to this situation. She could think of nothing specific to help the professor and his students. A small crowd had gathered at this point, in part to help Eric, in part to watch the comic situation unfolding. Eric was concerned that he not be injured, but he was also embarrassed by his predicament. Dan began to kid him, noting that maybe the young women at the college would "like his new look!"

Music teacher Lisette Deemer heard the commotion and came to offer Professor McClelland her help. Taking suggestions from the onlookers, the group tried pouring different substances over the mask, in an effort to loosen it from Eric's face. They poured water, cooking oil, and liquid soap on the mask, but nothing helped. Nothing would budge the mask. The suggestion was made to simply break the plaster, but Eric refused. He wasn't worried about getting hurt, but he felt that he had already suffered for this project—and he needed the credit for his art class! Professor McClelland offered to excuse him from the project, but Eric was adamant. He wanted the intact mask for a grade, and as a souvenir of his ordeal!

Now, unbeknownst to Eric, a call was placed to 911. Captain Gary Kuehn and two other firefighters quickly responded. Upon arrival they evaluated Eric's physical condition. When they had assured themselves that he was breathing easily and that his color was fine, they realized that they didn't have any equipment that could help free Eric's face. They suggested bringing Eric to the local hospital's emergency room, but Eric—fearing more laughter and embarrassment—declined their suggestion. Finally, someone suggested a dentist's office. Eric agreed to this solution; he knew that there would be fewer people at a dentist's office, and thus a smaller chance that anyone he knew would be there.

Eric and Dan carefully made their way to Professor McClelland's car, and he drove them to the offices of Lisette Deemer's dentist, Dr. Reinmuth. After looking over the situation, Dr. Reinmuth asked his office mate, orthodontist Dr. Dwornik, to help him. This made Eric nervous, because he had just broken up with Dr. Dwornik's daughter! Eric could only hope that Dr. Dwornik would behave professionally at all times!

The two doctors worked over Eric carefully, using their dental tools. They gently chipped away at the mask, beginning at Eric's hairline, where the mask seemed to be stuck. They tried to loosen the mask from his face, while at the same time leaving it as intact as possible, so that Eric could have his souvenir. It took them about forty-five minutes, but they were finally able to remove the mask from Eric's face. He

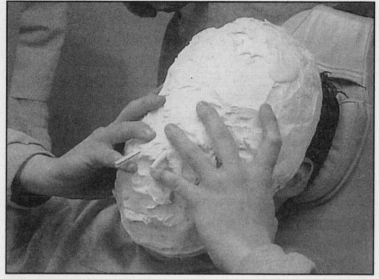

Eric struggles to pull the plaster mask off his face.

had a patch of red, inflamed skin on his forehead, where the plaster had been stuck, and some hair had been pulled from his scalp, but other than that he was fine. He suffered no permanent scars or damage.

However, he has had to put up with the teasing of his friends, and his legendary status on campus. Professor McClelland is relieved that no one was hurt. Eric says that one lesson he has learned is that an artist must carefully research the materials he is to use. Because they had not applied enough petroleum jelly to his forehead and hairline, the plaster stuck to his skin there. Dan notes that "all artists must suffer for their craft; Eric just suffered a little earlier and a little longer than most!"

Fascinating Facts

• Plaster of Paris cannot be used for objects that will be exposed to the weather, because it dissolves in water!

• Death masks are sometimes made to preserve the likenesses of people. Death masks exist for such famous people as Ludwig van Beethoven and Napoleon Bonaparte.

• Children all over the United States often wear masks on the last day of October every year—for Halloween!

Tongue-Tied

Who would ever think that camping equipment could be dangerous? Paul Benner certainly didn't—read on to discover another amusing rescue!

June 16, 1993, was a beautiful day in Union, Maine. It was sunny and hot, which suited the students at Union Elementary School just fine, since this was their annual school-wide Field Day. Special activities were planned throughout the day for the students and teachers. Right after recess, Charlyn Dickens, a teacher with over sixteen years experience, opened her classroom door and ushered her excited students back into her classroom. As most students flopped into their seats and began to fan themselves, nine-year-old Paul Benner brought his new gift—a

canteen—over to the faucet and filled it with
cold, clear water. He went back to his table,
where he offered a drink to his tablemates: Jon
Strout took a big swallow, then passed the canteen to their friend Carlton. Carlton also took a
swig, then handed the canteen back to Paul.
Paul leaned his head back and took a great big
gulp. When he tilted his head back down, however, the canteen didn't come away from his
mouth. Jon Strout remembers trying to make
sense of Paul's mumbled words, and thinking
that his friend was joking.

When it was clear to Jon that Paul really
couldn't remove the canteen from his mouth,
Jon called to his teacher, announcing that Paul
had "the canteen stuck on his tongue." Ms.
Dickens' reaction was one of amazement and
disbelief. As the class laughed, she made her
way over to Paul's table, where she tried to gently yank the canteen off his tongue. As she
twisted it just a bit, she could feel that the suc-
tion in the canteen was holding it fast to his
tongue. She could see that the threads on the
mouth of the canteen were stuck to Paul's
tongue. When the canteen didn't easily come
away, she decided that she needed help.

Asking her class to stay quiet and behave, she
left the room with Paul. Telling the boy to stay

calm, she flagged down a passing aide in the hallway. The aide walked with Paul and Ms. Dickens down to the school's gymnasium where the school's unofficial medic—gym teacher Mr. Lufkin—was supervising other Field Day activities. Mr. Lufkin is not a trained professional, but he knows the basic points to cover an emergency situation. Although the sight of Paul with a canteen stuck to his tongue was a comical one, Mr. Lufkin kept his composure and did not laugh. His first priority was to make sure that Paul could breathe; he could. Mr. Lufkin could see that Paul was starting to worry, so he reassured Paul and promised him that they'd get the canteen off his tongue.

Mr. Lufkin filled a sink in his office with ice. His plan was to have Paul stand over the sink with the canteen in the ice. He thought this would cool off the canteen and eventually cool off Paul's tongue. This would decrease any swelling in the tongue, and allow the canteen to slip off. Ms. Dickens, the aide, and Mr. Lufkin huddled around Paul, rubbing his back and taking turns trying to pull at the canteen. When they could see that the ice was having no effect, they decided to call 911.

Their call was received by the Maine State Police Department. When the dispatcher heard that help was needed to remove a canteen from a boy's tongue he chuckled and asked the caller to repeat himself. The dispatcher wanted to make sure he completely understood this crazy call! An alarm was then sent out to the Union Ambulance Corps. When EMT Pat McCallister heard the call, she was at home with her husband, Mike. After they listened to the dispatcher's message, Pat and Mike looked at each other and burst out laughing. Pat had been called to some strange emergencies, but this seemed the funniest of all!

When Pat and her partner arrived on the scene, Pat put on surgical gloves and used her fingers to try and back Paul's tongue out of the neck of the canteen. Her work had no effect, and she and her partner wondered what they should try next. In the meantime, Mike McCallister pulled up to the school in his van. Mike is a volunteer EMT and an electrician; he thought some of his equipment might come in handy.

At the same time, Paul's mother, Beth Benner, had heard of her son's plight, and came rushing to the school. The adults thought the situation was funny, but knew that it was also very serious. They worked together to keep Paul calm and to think of different ways to try and get his tongue free. Mike suggested drilling a

hole in the front of the canteen, at the point far-
thest away from Paul's tongue, to try and relieve some of the pressure in the canteen. He
thought that, if the canteen's vacuum was broken, Paul's tongue might just slip out of the canteen's neck.

With Beth Benner's approval, Mike began to
very carefully drill a hole through the top of the
canteen. When he was done, the adults again
tried to tug the canteen off of Paul's tongue.
When this didn't work, Mike tried blowing into
the hole he had made, hoping this would loosen
the threads' grip on Paul's tongue. Again Pat
used her fingers to try and back Paul's tongue
out of the opening. Pat and her partner knew
that because of various procedures they had
tried, Paul's tongue was beginning to swell.
They began to be concerned that the canteen
might work itself down onto the base of Paul's
tongue, where it could obstruct his airway. They
decided that they should get Paul to a hospital
as quickly as possible, so they called for an ambulance.

As they loaded Paul into the ambulance, students from Ms. Dickens' class, as well as other
students from the school, watched from the win-
dows. Jon Strout remembers thinking that, at
the hospital, doctors might need to cut off Paul's

tongue! So, while the sight of Paul with the canteen stuck to his face was funny, the students
also knew that this was a serious situation.
They were glad to know that Paul was being
taken care of by professionals, and they hoped
that he would be back in school very soon.

At the Penobscot Bay Medical Center, Emergency Room Nurse Charlotte Fowlie prepared
an examining room for Paul's arrival. She remembers thinking that she had plenty of experience with children sticking various objects in
their ears and noses, but she'd never had to help
someone with a stuck tongue before! When Paul
got to the hospital, Nurse Fowlie began by ap-
plying a lubricant to Paul's tongue. She hoped
that Paul's tongue would slip right out of the
opening. When this didn't work, she and the
surgeon on duty, Dr. Olaff Anderson, knew that
their only choice was to cut the canteen off. Dr.
Anderson thought to himself that he could probably give the canteen a great big yank and pull
it off Paul, but he thought that Paul's mother
would probably faint at the sight!

After Paul was given a mild sedative, Dr.
Anderson began snipping away at the canteen, using as his starting place the hole that
Mike McCallister had made. The canteen had
many metal seams, however, which made Dr.

Anderson's progress very slow. The delicate surgical instruments at his disposal, designed to work on a human body, weren't sturdy enough to cut through the metal canteen. So, Dr. Anderson called upon the engineering department at the hospital—a department with heavy-duty equipment. Using a pair of the engineering department's special shears, Dr. Anderson was able to move faster. He snipped in a straight line, right toward the mouth of the canteen—right toward Paul's tongue! As the shears got closer to Paul's mouth, Paul's mother told her son to take deep breaths and keep his eyes closed, so that he wouldn't have to watch. Finally, Dr. Anderson reached the neck of the canteen with the shears and made a final cut. The body of the canteen came away in his hands, leaving just a metal ring around Paul's tongue. Moving very carefully and slowly, Dr. Anderson made one more cut—the cut that freed Paul's tongue from the metal cylinder!

Everyone cheered and Paul began to smile. Dr. Anderson looked his tongue over carefully. The tongue was black and blue and swollen, but Dr. Anderson could not see any other damage. Paul was given a quick checkup, and a Popsicle, and then released. He was under orders to eat

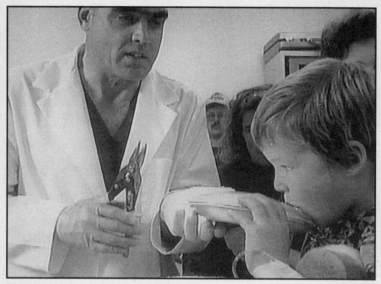

Dr. Olaff Anderson works carefully to remove the canteen from Paul's swollen tongue.

Popsicles, as the icy cold would relieve the swelling of his tongue!

Paul was able to return to school the next day, where he was greeted as a hero. He has vowed never to buy another canteen because you never know what might happen. His mother is glad that her son is safe and sound, and knows that he's learned his lesson—never stick your tongue where it doesn't belong!

Fascinating Facts

- Tongues may be ugly, but they help us to taste and swallow food—and to form words!

- Dogs and cats use their tongues to eat, to clean their fur, and to express affection.

- The ability to curl your tongue into a tube shape is inherited; if your parents can do it, you probably can too!

Headstrong or Stuck-Up?

When you call someone headstrong, you're calling them stubborn. When you say someone is stuck-up, you mean that they think they're better than you. So what would you call an animal that is both headstrong and stuck-up?

Saturday morning, November 17, 1990, dawned clear and beautiful in a quiet neighborhood in Shreveport, Louisiana. Richard White walked out his front door and down the path to his driveway. He was on his way to the nearby small town of Homer, where he was going to work. As he was about to get into his car, he heard a rustling and growling sound coming from one of the trees in his front yard. He looked up, searching through the leaves and branches for the source of the noise. He was

24

very surprised when he finally saw where the noise was coming from—there was a raccoon high up in one of his trees.

Richard knew that raccoons are nocturnal animals—which means they are active at night and sleep during the day—so he thought there was something strange about this raccoon being out and about in broad daylight. As he continued to look at the raccoon and wonder about its appearance, he noticed another startling fact: The raccoon's head was in a hole in one of the dead limbs of the tree. As Richard watched, he could tell that the raccoon's head was *stuck* in the hole, and that the animal was struggling to get it out. Not sure what to do, Richard went back into his house and called for his wife, Rhonda, to see what she thought of the situation.

Rhonda immediately saw that the raccoon would not be able to free itself. It was clinging to the branch and trying to pull its head out, with no luck. Richard and Rhonda could hear the sounds of the raccoon's claws on the branch, and could hear it growling and whining. The animal would scratch and try to free itself, then give up in exhaustion and simply dangle high above the ground, all four of its legs clearly visible. Although it was a comical sight, Rhonda and Richard knew that the raccoon could not survive much longer in the tree. If it continued to dangle there by its neck, it would surely die. They did not want to let that happen, so Rhonda thought fast and made a quick call to 911.

The 911 dispatcher who answered Rhonda's call listened to her description of the animal in the tree with sympathy, but told her that 911 could not dispatch a fire-fighting team. The 911 dispatcher advised Rhonda to call Animal Control, and wished her luck. Rhonda called Animal Control, who told her that they didn't have the proper equipment to get to the animal, since it was trapped so high up in the tree.

With nowhere else to turn, Rhonda and Richard were getting desperate. They really wanted to save this raccoon, which they had nicknamed Rocky! As Rhonda later stated, she and Richard believe that human beings have a responsibility to the other creatures on this earth. So, as funny as the raccoon may have looked—way up in the tree with its head stuck in a dead limb—the Whites could not turn their backs. Having tried all the official avenues for help, Rhonda and Richard decided to call her father, Ted Griffin. Mr. Griffin is a retired landscaper, and had at his disposal a very tall ladder, a saw, and some ropes. When he heard

"Rocky" dangles, helpless and exhausted, from the tree limb high above ground.

what they were calling about, he thought that the raccoon had gotten itself into a pretty humorous situation. But he knew that his daughter and son-in-law were serious, and that they needed his help. He agreed to come to their house as quickly as he could. He loaded up his equipment and rushed off to the White house, about a ten-minute drive away.

In the meantime, Reggie Hargrove, one of the Whites' neighbors, was leaving his house to play a round of golf at a local course. When he saw all of the commotion in the Whites' front yard, he

dropped his golf bag and clubs and ran over to
lend a hand. Reggie saw how serious the Whites
were about getting the raccoon free. He also saw
that someone could get badly hurt if they
weren't careful. Richard White had already
climbed the lower section of the tree, and was
trying to get as close to the raccoon as possible.
Reggie recommended that Rhonda call 911.
When Rhonda told him that she already had,
and that the 911 dispatcher had been unable to
help, and that Animal Control had been unable
to help, Reggie volunteered to call 911 again. He
knew that he had to convince a rescue crew to
come to the house, since one of Rocky's rescuers
was likely to be injured if professional help
didn't arrive soon!

Just as Reggie was going into the Whites'
house to make the phone call, Ted Griffin drove
up with a car full of equipment. As Reggie
watched from inside the house, Ted set up his
ladder and climbed up to join his son-in-law in
the tree. When Reggie reached 911 dispatcher
Kathy Salter, he explained the situation. He
said that, although they had been advised that
a 911 rescue team could not respond to an animal rescue, several neighbors were now trying
to climb the tree and rescue the raccoon. Children from the neighborhood had begun to

gather to watch the progress of the rescue. As Reggie explained to the dispatcher, there was a potential for injuries if a rescue team didn't help soon. When he described Ted Griffin, a man in his seventies, climbing a ladder to a limb high above the ground, the dispatcher agreed to send a rescue team. The dispatcher knew that the 911 crew had to keep the *humans* from hurting themselves! On the ground, Rhonda White remembers seeing her father climb up the ladder and thinking that, if her mother could see him, she'd really be mad! Reggie watched Richard in the tree, and thought that Richard had lost his priorities: He had a bad back and was endangering his own life to help a wild raccoon!

When Fire Chief Charles Scarborough received the call to help a raccoon in a tree, he laughed. He remembers thinking that that's exactly where raccoons belong—in trees! When he arrived at the scene, however, he put in a call for an aerial truck. The aerial truck was necessary to get high enough up in the tree. This call was unique; Chief Scarborough and his crew had often been called upon to get cats out of trees. As he noted later, however, the difference between this call and a cat-in-a-tree call is that a cat will eventually come down. He remembers asking one distraught cat owner, whose cat was "stuck" in a tree, if she had ever seen a cat skeleton in a tree. When she replied that she had never seen such a thing, he pointed out to her that this is because a cat *can* get out of a tree—when it's good and ready. In this case, however, he knew the raccoon was stuck fast, and that they'd have to get it free as quickly as possible.

When the aerial fire truck arrived, Ted Griffin and Richard White climbed down from the tree and let the professionals climb up to do their jobs. They both knew that raccoons can be dangerous, and were happy to see the fire-fighting team. The firefighters made their way up to the dead, hollow limb where the raccoon was caught. Since there was no way they could pull the raccoon's head out of the hole, they decided to cut the whole tree limb off. Using a powerful chain saw, they very carefully cut the limb off the trunk of the tree. Then, with the raccoon still dangling by its neck, the two firefighters made their way back down the ladder, carrying the limb between them.

Once on the ground, they gently laid the limb and raccoon on the grass. The raccoon showed signs of being very weak—it had stopped digging at the wood with its claws, and its growls and whines were softer and less frequent. The firefighters decided that the only way they could release the raccoon was if they split the hollow limb like a piece of firewood. The dead limb on the ground was about six feet in length, with the raccoon's head stuck right in the middle. Working carefully, they drove a hatchet into one side of the hollow limb, and used a large mallet to force the hatchet's blade deeper into the wood. As one of the firefighters, wearing heavy gloves, held the raccoon's body, they worked on the limb. The split in the wood got closer and closer to the raccoon's head, until it was finally free!

With the animal free, the firefighter picked the raccoon up and held it in front of him at chest height, away from his body. The neighbors applauded. The firefighter quickly crossed the street, where he planned to deposit the raccoon in the woods. On his way across the street, however, the raccoon turned and began to bite his gloved hand! At that, the firefighter gently tossed the animal a few feet onto the soft ground of the woods. The raccoon got right to its feet and scampered away through the trees. The neighborhood children tried to keep it in sight, but it was too quick for them. The last they saw of the animal was it scrambling up another tree!

Richard and Rhonda White are happy that they were able to fulfill the obligation they felt, and safely get the raccoon down from the tree. They believe that the neighborhood children learned a valuable lesson about the responsibilities we have to all of the earth's creatures. They just hope that Rocky is more careful in the future!

Fascinating Facts

- The American Society for the Prevention of Cruelty to Animals (the ASPCA) was formed in 1866 to help all animals, whether domesticated or wild.

- Raccoons are nocturnal animals. Other nocturnal animals are bats, owls, and mice.

- In the 1830s and 1840s, the Whig Party in the United States used the raccoon as its emblem.

Potty Peril

You'd never think that using the bathroom could be dangerous to your health, would you? One little girl found out the truth the hard way. Read on for more funny details!

On a quiet summer day—July 7, 1992—in Port St. Lucie, Florida, Kristine Cole was watching television. The two-and-a-half-year-old was home with her older brother, her baby brother, her mother, and a neighborhood girl who was helping her mother watch the three children. Mrs. Cole describes young Kristine as mischievous and full of fun; her older brother describes her as "being a pain" sometimes, and "bossy" other times. Both agree that Kristine is a fun and active little girl. While baby-sitter Melissa McAvoy watched Kristine and her older brother, Mrs. Cole held the baby and talked on the telephone.

During one commercial break in her television show, Kristine skipped into the kitchen and told her mother that she had to use the potty. The Coles were in the middle of toilet-training Kristine, so Mrs. Cole told the child to go on ahead into the bathroom, and that she would join Kristine as soon as she got off the telephone. As Mrs. Cole was wrapping up her telephone conversation, she heard Kristine calling to her from the bathroom. Mrs. Cole called for Melissa. When Melissa appeared in the kitchen doorway, Mrs. Cole asked her to check on Kristine, and see what was the matter. Melissa hurried to the bathroom, and was met with an astonishing sight: Kristine had her foot stuck in the toilet bowl!

Melissa remembers being very surprised to find the little girl with her foot in the toilet. She tried not to laugh, because she could see that Kristine was upset. Murmuring comforting words, she plunged her hands into the water in the toilet bowl and attempted to free Kristine's foot. When that didn't work, and Kristine kept calling for her mother, Melissa gave up and went to fetch Mrs. Cole from the kitchen. She explained what had happened.

Mrs. Cole was dumbfounded: She remembers thinking, "How can a foot go into a toilet and not come out?" She rushed with Melissa back into the bathroom, where they took turns comforting Kristine and trying to pull her foot out of the toilet. When it became obvious that just pulling wasn't going to work, they decided to pour dish-washing liquid into the toilet bowl. They thought the slippery soap might coat Kristine's foot and allow it to slip out. Unfortunately, Kristine's foot was wedged in so tightly that the dish-washing liquid did not work. Mrs. Cole began to worry about pulling on Kristine's leg; she wasn't sure whether the blood circulation to Kristine's foot had been cut off, and she wanted to make sure they didn't break a bone in her leg or foot.

When she was sure there was nothing else they could try, Mrs. Cole dialed 911 for help. The dispatcher on duty listened to Mrs. Cole, and then asked her to repeat herself. Mrs. Cole remembers the dispatcher hesitating when she explained that her little girl's foot was stuck in the toilet. She told the dispatcher, "I know it sounds crazy, but it's really true!" She knew that the dispatcher had doubts as to whether she was serious!

The call went out and Port St. Lucie/Fort

Pierce Fire Rescue units responded immediately. Records show that rescue crews were on the scene within six minutes! One of the respondents was a six-year veteran paramedic named Andy MacDonald. Mr. MacDonald remembers thinking that this was no routine call, so it was bound to be interesting! The head of the rescue unit, Lieutenant Larry Barton, thought that the situation might look funny, but that it was very serious. He knew that the small child would be frightened by feeling trapped and helpless.

Larry, Andy, and the rest of the rescue unit crowded into the bathroom and worked on trying to free Kristine's foot. When it became obvious that their efforts weren't helping, Larry called on the only "toilet expert" he knew: Captain Bill Davis. Mr. Davis had worked in construction for many years, so Larry knew that he would know how to work with this toilet. Mr. Davis was contacted in his car via the fire department radio; when he heard what was going on, the only advice he could give the rescue crew was to unbolt and detach the toilet from the bathroom wall, carry it outside, and wait for his arrival.

Mrs. Cole remembers being surprised by this development. She had assumed that when she

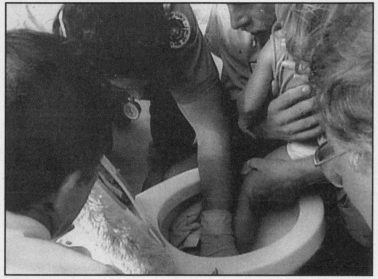

Anxious rescue workers struggle to free Kristine's foot.

called 911, she would find people who knew more about toilets than she did. She never expected to have her bathroom dismantled before her eyes, or that her toilet would end up out on the driveway! Kristine's older brother remembers that Kristine was screaming and crying because she was afraid of the strangers in her family's bathroom. He thought that all the neighbors on the block could probably hear her yelling!

Meanwhile, John Cole had been working in the neighborhood, and just happened to stop by his house to see how his family was doing. He never expected to see rescue trucks in front of his house! On his way up the driveway, he was met by Kristine's older brother, who quickly explained the situation. Mr. Cole rushed into his bathroom to find his hysterical daughter, worried wife, and a crowd of rescue workers. The rescuers explained that their instructions were to detach the toilet from the wall. Mr. Cole tried to comfort Kristine as best he could while the crew worked on the plumbing.

When all of the screws had been loosened and the bolts undone, the crew was able to lift the toilet from the wall. Then, while Mr. Cole safely held onto Kristine, they carefully carried the toilet—with its reluctant passenger—out into the driveway. Lieutenant Barton remembers thinking, "OK, we've got the child and the toilet in the driveway, *now* what do we do?" Fortunately, at that moment, Captain Davis pulled into the driveway. Captain Davis, the plumbing authority, advised the crew to stuff towels around Kristine's foot, so that when they broke the toilet, none of the pieces of porcelain would hurt her. Towels were brought out from the house and jammed into the toilet bowl surrounding the little girl's foot.

When they had made her foot as secure as

possible, they began chipping away at the back of the toilet. Using the pick end of a pry axe, one of the crew members carefully chipped at the neck of the toilet. When they were able to break a piece off, however, they discovered that they were too far away from Kristine's foot, and that they would have to keep chipping. With a few more deliberately aimed blows, they were finally able to break apart the toilet enough to free Kristine.

When the last piece holding her captive had been chipped away, Kristine leaped into her father's arms and immediately stopped crying. The rescue team packed up their equipment, loaded up their truck, and drove slowly away from the house, all the time exchanging waves with the now-smiling Kristine. The little girl came out of the ordeal with only a minor cut on her foot. Her parents are delighted to report that she successfully finished her potty-training with no other setbacks. They will allow that they view their bathroom differently now, but they know that, with children, anything can happen!

Fascinating Facts

- During the Middle Ages, people in Europe disposed of their wastes by throwing them into the streets!

- In the 1860s, Sir Thomas Crapper, an English plumber, made improvements on an existing flush toilet and created the modern toilets that we all use today.

- A palace built on the island of Crete nearly 4,000 years ago had primitive toilets and a drainage system using air shafts for vents.